All About
TOUCH

All About

TOUCH

by Irene Bates
Illustrated by Jill Newton

Thameside Press

Distributed in the United States by
Smart Apple Media
1980 Lookout Drive
North Mankato, MN 56003

Illustrations copyright © Jill Newton

ISBN 1-931983-01-1

Library of Congress Control Number 2002 141353

Series editor: Maria O'Neill
Series designer: Hayley Cove

Printed by Midas, Hong Kong

Contents

What is touch?

You have five senses. They are hearing, taste, smell, sight and touch. Explore the world around you using touch.

Touch is about feeling things. Close your eyes. Touch lots of things with your fingertips. Do they all feel the same?

When you touch the surface
of something, you can feel
whether it is smooth or
rough, knobbly or furry.
This is texture.

Look at all the textures
on this texture wheel.
Can you name them?

Which one looks
smooth? Which one
looks prickly? Which
looks spongy? Which looks
rough? Which looks furry?
Which looks knobbly?

More about touch

Touch something and feel its texture. Now decide if it is hot or cold. Is it wet or dry? Is it hard or soft?

If you touch a pizza, it feels soft and spongy. You can eat it hot or cold.

This dog has been swimming. His fur feels wet and cold.

The rough bark on this tree feels hard and dry.

When you drink hot chocolate, it feels smooth and wet.

Hard and soft

Touch something hard. Feel your finger squash against it. Soft things squash when you touch them.

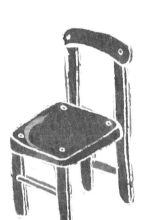

Look at the things on these pages. Which ones would be soft to touch? Which ones would be hard?

The shell of an egg is hard. When you crack the egg open, the inside is soft.

Lips are soft. Teeth are hard so you can bite and chew food.

Make a snail

Use modeling clay to make your own snail. Feel how soft the clay is in your hands. When you leave the clay snail to set, it gets hard.

Snails have hard shells that protect them from danger.

Wet and dry

Wet things feel moist and slimy. When they are dry, they feel very different.

How many wet things can you see here? Which ones are always wet? Count the dry things on these pages. Which ones can you eat?

Make lentil mud

Pour dried lentils into a bowl. What do they feel like? Fill the bowl with water. Leave the lentils for 30 minutes. What do they feel like now?

Look out of the window on a rainy day. Outside, everything is wet, but you stay warm and dry.

Snakes look wet, but their skin is dry when you touch it.

Plants need lots of water to drink. If you leave them without water, they dry up and die.

Hot and cold

Ice cubes feel cold. The weather on a sunny summer day is hot. Most things can be hot or cold.

Name the things on these pages that are too hot to touch. Which ones are really cold? Which things are not too hot or too cold?

Inside your fridge the cold air keeps food fresh.

Deserts are very hot, dry places.

Go for a swim
Ask an adult to take you swimming. When you jump in the water, you feel very cold. How do you feel after swimming for five minutes?

The ice at a skating rink is kept frozen at all times.

Rough

**Touch a rough surface
with your fingertips.
Feel how uneven
and rugged it is.**

Look at all the things on
these pages. Would you be
able to feel their texture
with your toes?

Make a rough surface

Press some modeling clay over the surface of something rough. How does the clay feel when you take it away?

Most animals have rough tongues.

Some people climb ropes. They can grip the rope because it has a rough surface.

When mud dries on your shoes, it feels rough.

Smooth

Smooth things have no wrinkles or uneven parts. You can slide your fingers along a smooth surface.

How many smooth things can you see here? Do smooth things feel good to touch?

Polish an apple to make it very smooth and shiny.

Collect smooth leaves

Pick some shiny leaves and petals. Feel how smooth they are. Leave them in a warm place for two days. How do they feel now?

Spoons feel smooth. Use a spoon to eat a smooth yogurt.

Babies have very smooth skin. How smooth does your skin feel?

Prickly

Some plants and animals have prickles. Some things made by people are prickly too.

Can you name the prickly things on these pages? Which ones can you eat? Which one is an animal?

Porcupines
have spines
that stand up
at the first
sign of danger.

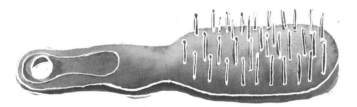

Fir trees have pine
needles that are
very prickly.

If you touch something
sharp, your brain
says "ouch"!

A prickly project
Look for things that feel
prickly or bristly. Can
you find pins and needles,
a hairbrush, a doormat
with stiff bristles?

Spongy

Spongy things are soft. When you squeeze them, they spring back into shape.

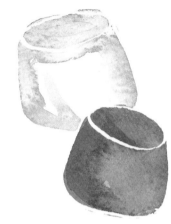

Find things that you can squeeze like the ones on these pages. Close your eyes and touch the things. Can you tell which is which?

A spongy collection

Collect ten things that are spongy or squashy. How many of these can you eat? How many do you use for washing?

This foam mat is spongy. It protects the athlete when he lands.

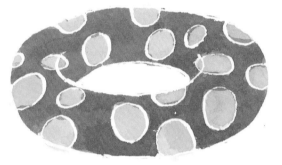

Rubber rings are spongy. They help you float on water.

You can have lots of fun with sponges in the bathtub. Natural sponges grow on the seabed.

Knobbly

Knobbly things have bumps and lumps. Some knobbly things are smooth, others are rough.

Name the things on these pages that are smooth and knobbly. Which ones are rough and knobbly?

Blind people read special raised dots with their fingertips. The dots make up letters. This is called braille.

The huge tires on this tractor are black and knobbly.

Knobbly rubbings
Find five things that feel knobbly. Press paper on each one and crayon over the surface. Make five knobbly rubbings.

If you crack open these knobbly shells, you will find nuts inside.

Furry

Many animals are covered in thick hair called fur. Lots of other things feel furry too.

Can you name all the things on these pages that would feel furry? Why do they feel good to touch?

A hairy project
Put an ice cube on your arm. What happens to the hairs? Nature protects you from the cold by making your hairs stand on end.

A fluffy bathmat feels soft and furry.

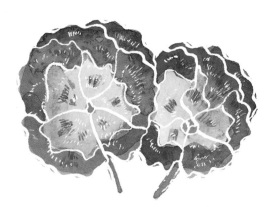

The petals on these pansies are yellow and blue. They feel furry.

Baby birds have soft, fluffy feathers called down.

Explore touch

Make a furry ball

1 Cut out two card circles. Now cut a hole in the center of each one.
2 Press the circles together. Wind wool around them.
3 Cut through the wool at the edge of the circles.
4 Loop wool between the circles and tie a knot.
5 Now take away the card circles.

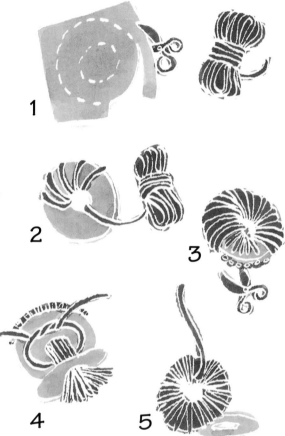

Which feels warmest?

Find a white cloth and a black cloth. Leave them in the sunshine for an hour. Which cloth feels warmest?

Touching game

Find some things like these.
Ask a friend to close her eyes
and touch the things with
her fingertips. Then ask her
to give a touch or texture
word to describe each one.

Picture list

Here is a list of the pictures in this book.

Hard and soft   Chair, nuts, wool, lamb, banana, spade, armchair, egg, lips, teeth, snails.

Wet and dry   Dry hair, wet washing, crackers, faucet, wet hair, watermelon, dried apricots, tongue, rainy day, snake, flowers being watered, flowers without water.

Hot and cold   Sun, salad, soup, drink with ice cubes, snowy mountains, hot drink, warm bath, fridge, fire, desert, ice cream, lollipop, ice skaters.

Rough   Shells, coconut, kiwi fruit, brick wall, elephant, doormat, tree bark, cow and cow's tongue, rope, bread roll, toast, muddy shoes.

Smooth Book, mirror, beach ball, spaghetti with sauce, car, pepper, silk dress, apple, spoon and yogurt, umbrella, baby, marbles.

Prickly Thistle, cactuses, holly leaves, pineapple, blackberries, needle and thread, porcupine, fir tree, hairbrush, pins and needles, chestnut.

Spongy Marshmallows, ball, toy giraffe, cushion, ripe tomato, bed, cake, high jumper, rubber ring, sandwich, sponges.

Knobbly Starfish, calculator, corn on the cob, table tennis paddle, crocodile, toy brick, braille, tractor, knot in rope, cauliflower, peanuts.

Furry Teddy bear, dandelion seed head, caterpillar, paintbrush, rabbit, mohair sweater, bathmat, peach, pansies, owlets, furry slippers.

Words to remember

braille a special pattern of raised dots. Blind people read these dots with their fingertips. (see page 25)

danger something that may harm you.
(see pages 11, 21)

protect keep safe from harm. (see page 11)

seabed the bottom of the sea. (see page 23)

senses you have five senses. These are touch, taste, smell, sight and hearing. Your senses give you information about the world around you.
(see page 6)

surface the outside of something. (see pages 7, 16–18, 25)

texture what you feel when you touch the surface of something. (see pages 7–8, 16)